PHOTOGRAPHIC HIGHLIGHTS OF

The Peak District

BRADWELL
BOOKS

ABOUT

THE PEAK DISTRICT

For those of you who are not familiar with the Peak District it is a large area in the north of Derbyshire, bounded by Cheshire, Greater Manchester, Staffordshire and South and West Yorkshire. Most of the area falls within the Peak District National Park, which was designated as the United Kingdom's first national park in 1951.

The area is divided into the northern, Dark Peak, which is mainly moorland with gritstone outcrops, and the southern, White Peak, where much of the population lives and the geology is mainly limestone-based. The South West Peak is not so well known but has equally dramatic views of moors punctuated by outcrops of rock, rivers and woodland.

ANDREW

Has worked as a graphic designer in advertising for over thirty years. His patience and attention to detail is reflected in the quality of his landscape photography. When he met Sue in 1996 they realised that they shared a love of the countryside, and since then they have spent many weekends exploring the trails and remote areas of the Peak District National Park. In addition to photography Andy is also a keen

badminton player, an accomplished cook and somehow manages to read the odd science fiction book.

Equipment used:
Camera: *Canon 7D*
Lens: *Canon EF 17-40mm f/4L Ultra Wide Angle*
Processing: *Apple iMac 27" 2.7 GHz quad-core, running Photoshop CS5*

SUSAN

Is a hairdresser and has two grown up children, Nicola and Simon. Her enthusiasm for photography began in 2001 when she acquired a small film camera, and in 2006 she progressed to digital imagery. Fortunate to live so close to the Peak District, she and Andy are able to hike most weekends. She has absorbed many of Andy's photographic tips and skills, so there is now a friendly rivalry over who can get the best

shots! Sue ensures she is fit enough for all the hiking by taking regular Pilates classes in her free time.

Equipment used:
Camera: *Canon 20D*
Lens: *Canon EF-S 18-55mm f/3.5-f/5.6*

PHOTOGRAPHIC HIGHLIGHTS OF

The Peak District

To Susan, Christmas 2012 love from Ada x

A BOOK BY
ANDREW & SUSAN CAFFREY

BRADWELL
BOOKS

Published by Bradwell Books
9 Orgreave Close Sheffield S13 9NP
Email: books@bradwellbooks.co.uk
©Andrew & Susan Caffrey 2012

British Library Cataloguing in Publication Data:
a catalogue record for this book is available from
the British Library.

1st Edition
ISBN: 9781902674407
Print: Gomer Press, Llandysul, Ceredigion SA44 4JL

Copywriting by: Louise Maskill
Design by: Andrew Caffrey

CONTENTS

INTRODUCTION

JOIN US as we guide you through our portfolio of Peak District photographs. Sue and I work as a team; we are both enthusiastic walkers and photographers, but this is no ordinary partnership. As we walk through the landscape we take it in turns to keep an eye on the weather, while the other is looking for the next shot.

Capturing some of these images has been a test of patience and endurance, returning year after year to the same places to get that perfect shot of a particular vista. We have even been known to simply lie face down on the ground and wait for the clouds to disappear or the sunlight to glance an outcrop of rock to give it that perfect hue.

With images covering everything from deep wide valleys and narrow steep gorges to gently rolling hills and dramatic rocky outcrops, the collection shows the Peak District in all its seasons and moods. We have walked through this delightful landscape time and again, ready to capture the views that we love and for you to enjoy in this book. Duly inspired, we hope that we might encourage you to visit some of the places you have seen on these pages.

CASTLETON

ALONG THE GREAT
RIDGE FROM MAM TOR

The late medieval ruins of Peveril Castle dominate
Castleton's southern skyline. The village's four
show caves, one accessible only by boat, were
created during the area's lead-mining past.
Derbyshire Blue John, a unique semi-precious
mineral, is only found in the Castleton area,
and is still highly sought-after for decorative use.

CASTLETON

BUTTERTON

A WALK ON THE MANIFOLD WAY

The Staffordshire village of Butterton lies on the Manifold Way, formerly a light railway and now a walking and cycling route across the Peaks. In the centre of Butterton the Hoo Brook crosses a road, creating a small ford. Nearby Ecton Hill is riddled with the remains of ancient copper and lead mines, evidence of an industrial past.

CURBAR EDGE

A GRITSTONE RIDGE IN THE HEART OF THE DERBYSHIRE DALES

Popular with rock-climbers and walkers alike, the dramatic gritstone outcrop of Curbar Edge forms a barrier between the high eastern moors and the lower lands of Derwent Dale to the west. The area is rich in history, with ancient field systems and cairns as well as abandoned millstones providing evidence of man's activities at this beautiful spot.

CURBAR EDGE

DOVEDALE

IN THE VALLEY OF
THE RIVER DOVE

Dovedale, a three-mile valley cut by the River
Dove, is a nature reserve noted for its caves and
spectacular limestone formations as well as its
rich wildlife. It is one of the most popular walking
routes in Derbyshire, with footpaths running
alongside the river and taking in the iconic
stepping stones below Thorpe Cloud.

FOOLOW

A BEAUTIFUL TRADITIONAL LIMESTONE VILLAGE

Eyam is famously known as the Derbyshire plague village, which chose to isolate itself when plague broke out there in 1665. Less than a quarter of the villagers survived the disease. The upland countryside between Eyam and the neighbouring village of Foolow is beautiful, with rich pasture bordered by miles of drystone walls.

EDALE

THE START OF
THE PENNINE WAY

For serious walkers, the Old Nag's Head in the
village of Edale is the official start of the Pennine
Way. Edale itself is the site of a historic cotton
mill, part of the Peak District's rich industrial
heritage, and is surrounded by spectacular
countryside from Kinder Scout in the north to
Mam Tor and Win Hill in the south and east.

EDALE

ELTON

WHERE LIMESTONE AND GRITSTONE MEET

Robin Hood's Stride is a spectacular gritstone tor
perched on a ridge near the village of Elton.
Legend has it that Robin Hood strode between
the two spires of the outcrop – unlikely since
they're 15m apart! The area is rich in history, with
a Hermit's Cave and a variety of Bronze Age
remains including the Nine Stones Close circle.

ASHFORD IN THE WATER

ON THE BANKS OF THE RIVER WYE

Like many Derbyshire villages, Ashford in the Water is known for its late Spring tradition of well-dressing, as well as for the quarrying of Ashford Black marble. The Sheepwash Bridge crosses the River Wye here, its name commemorating the shepherding practice of washing sheep by swimming them across the river before shearing.

THE
ROACHES

SPECTACULAR GRITSTONE
ROCK FORMATIONS

The Roaches, a prominent gritstone ridge above Leek and Tittesworth Reservoir, is a mecca for climbers and walkers. It has spectacular rock formations, panoramic views of Cheshire and beyond (on a clear day one can even glimpse Snowdon), and if you're really lucky you might even spot a wallaby!

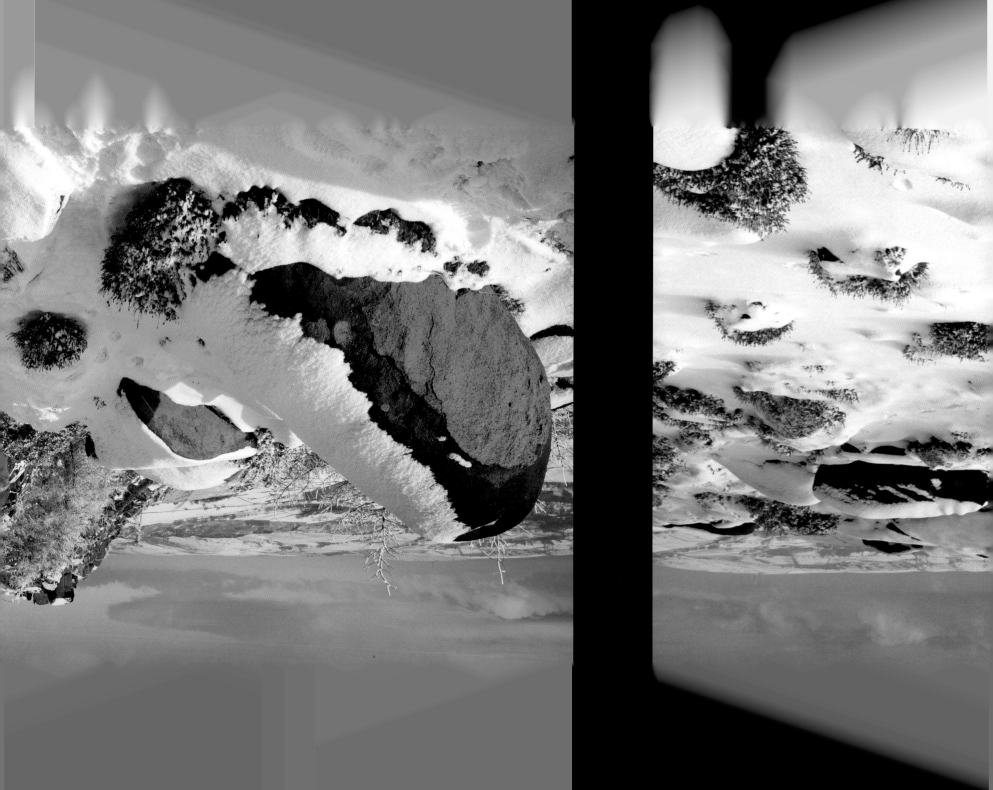

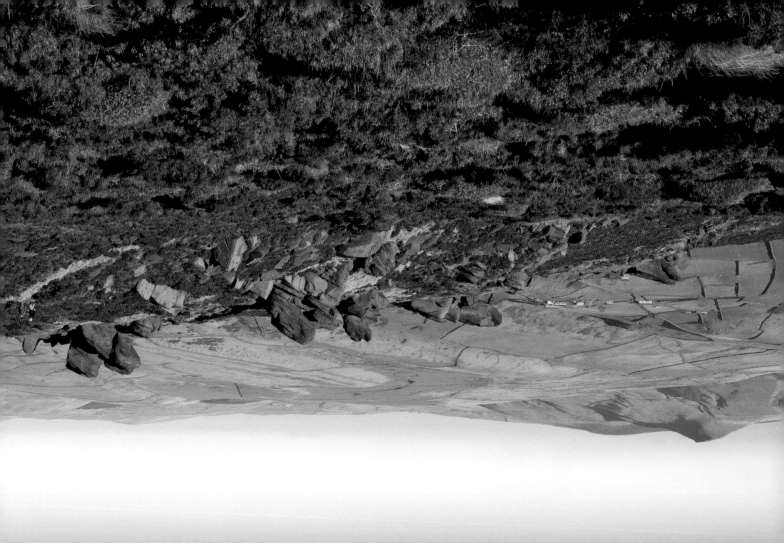

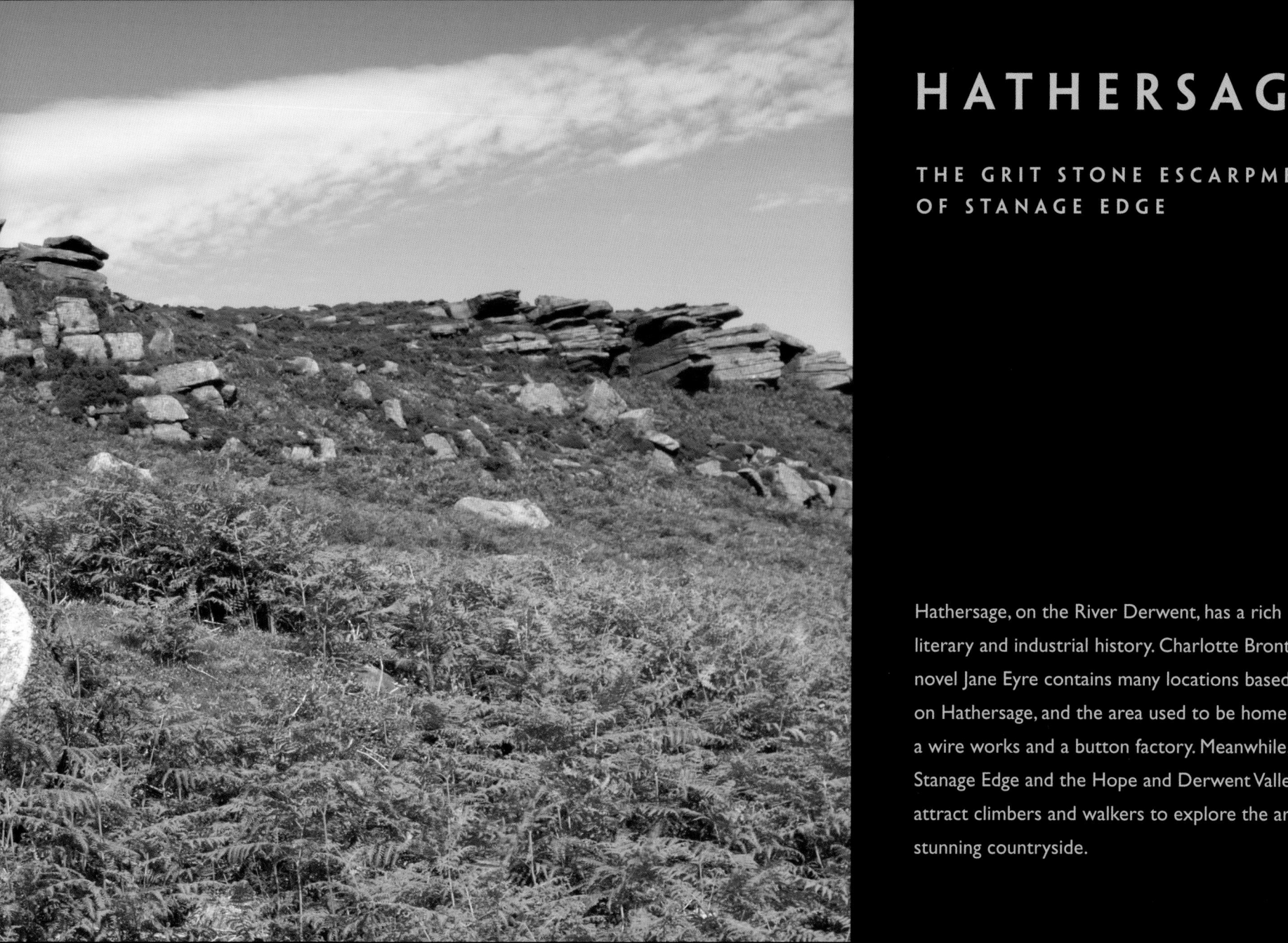

HATHERSAGE

THE GRIT STONE ESCARPMENT OF STANAGE EDGE

Hathersage, on the River Derwent, has a rich
literary and industrial history. Charlotte Bronte's
novel Jane Eyre contains many locations based
on Hathersage, and the area used to be home to
a wire works and a button factory. Meanwhile,
Stanage Edge and the Hope and Derwent Valleys
attract climbers and walkers to explore the area's
stunning countryside.

THE GOYT VALLEY

MOORS AND VALLEYS ON THE DERBYSHIRE/CHESHIRE BORDER

The River Goyt rises high on Axe Edge Moor and flows north, creating the spectacular and romantic Goyt Valley as it does so. The valley is bursting with history as well as natural beauty, with the Victorian ruins of Errwood Hall, industrial remains from quarrying and manufacture, and the modern Fernilee and Errwood reservoirs.

GOYT VALLEY

GOYT VALLEY

LATHKILL DALE

THE MOST BEAUTIFUL LIMESTONE DALE

Lathkill Dale is one of the finest limestone dales in the Peaks. Now a nature reserve, it has a history of lead mining and the remains of the ancient Mandale Mine can still be seen among the trees. The River Lathkill itself is unusually clear and renowned for its trout, with numerous fishponds near the medieval Conksbury Bridge.

LATHKILL DALE

THREE SHIRES HEAD

A MEETING OF THREE COUNTIES

An ancient packhorse bridge spans the waterfalls of the River Dane at Three Shires Head, the spot on Axe Edge Moor where the counties of Cheshire, Staffordshire and Derbyshire meet. Four trade routes once converged here, carrying silk from Hollinsclough and coal from the surrounding moorland to the industrial centre at Macclesfield.

THREE SHIRES HEAD

THREE SHIRES HEAD

THREE SHIRES HEAD

GRINDON

A GRITSTONE VILLAGE
IN THE MANIFOLD VALLEY

The gritstone village of Grindon has a fine
parish church with an elegant spire, known as
"the Cathedral of the Moorlands". The village
stands in the Manifold Valley, with the Manifold Way
(formerly the route of the Leek and Manifold Light
Railway) running close by and attracting walkers and
cyclists to this beautiful corner of Staffordshire.

GRINDON

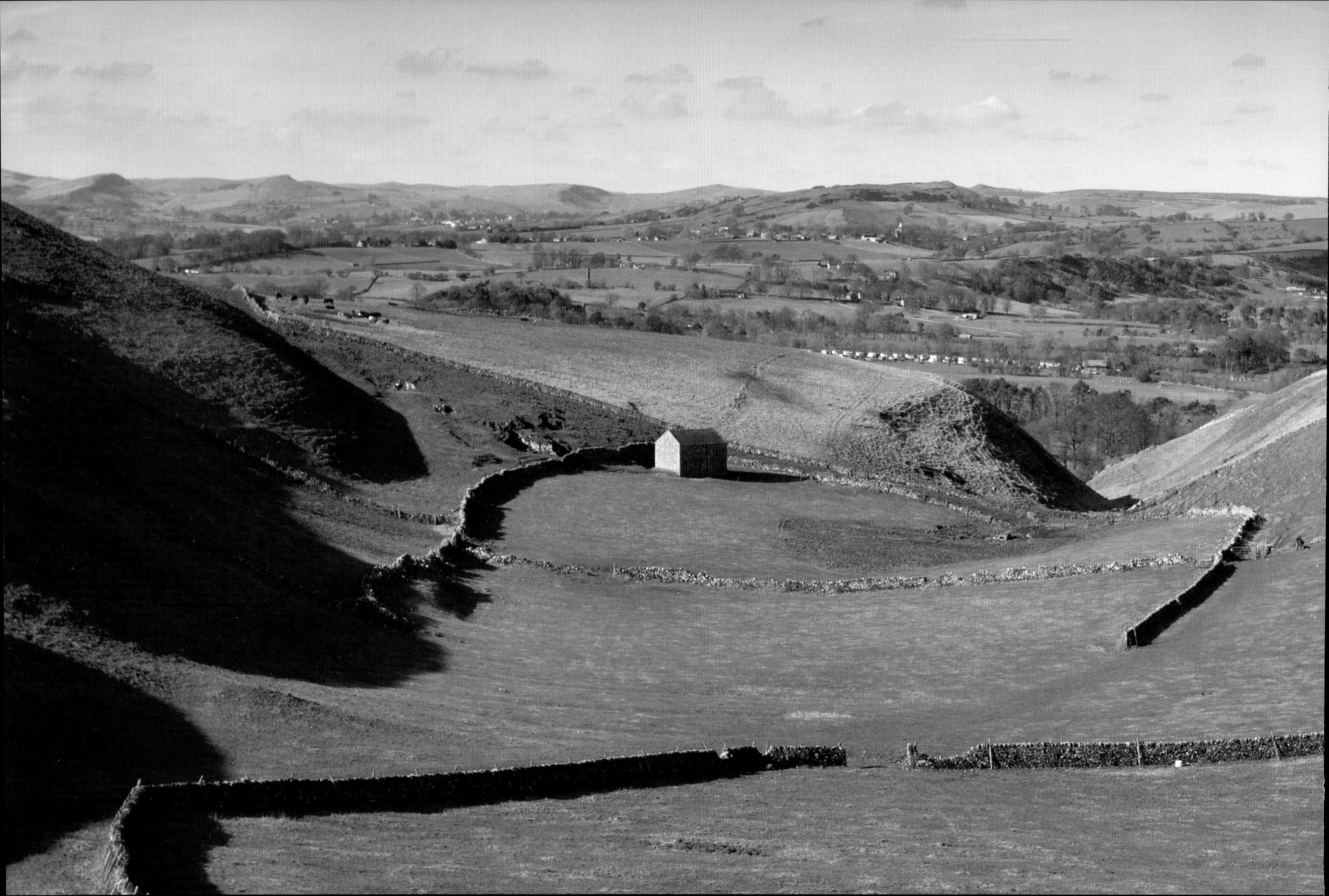

HARTINGTON

BY THE RIVER DOVE

Two cycling and walking routes, the Tissington and High Peak Trails, meet near the village of Hartington. The village lies on the River Dove, and the surrounding area has many medieval and Neolithic remains. The area used to be known for mining and cheese production, with the village creamery still supplying locally made cheeses.

TIDESWELL

IN THE SHADOW OF THE CATHEDRAL OF THE PEAK

Tideswell *(known locally as Tidza)* is the second largest settlement in the Peaks after Bakewell. It has a proud history of wool-trading and lead-mining, but these days it is best known for its magnificent fourteenth-century parish church, called the Cathedral of the Peak. The village's famous well-dressings take place in June, attracting tourists and locals alike.

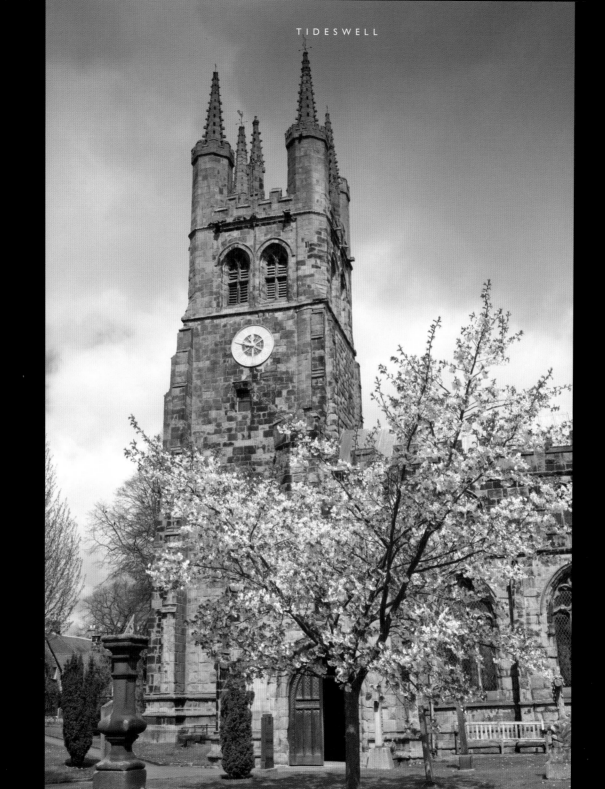

INTO THE SUNSET...

Our photography has taken us on a journey that has been both challenging and rewarding. There have been lows, when we wondered whether the discomfort of near frostbite was really worth the effort but these were far outweighed by the highs, back home in the warmth, seeing the results on screen or occasionally in a publication.

But here and now in these pages we are thrilled that the people at Bradwell Books have had the confidence to let us put together this beautiful book to share our work with you.

We have a vast portfolio, and we hope to be compiling more books in years to come.

Susan & Andrew Caffrey